Seven uni-verses

Poetry on all that space evokes

Jatan Mehta

Cover picture: A contrasting view of the total lunar eclipse of September 7, 2025 as seen from Bangalore, India. Image: Jatan Mehta

Seven uni-verses

Poetry on all that space evokes

“Best read looking up at our Moon, and the planets & stars”

Jatan Mehta

jatan.space

ISBN: 9789334432558

See the **About** and **Accessibility** pages for pamphlet and ownership details.

ISBNs of this book's formats

- Ebook: 9789334418880
- Print International: 9789334432558
- Print India: 9789334448832
- Audiobook: 9789334434989

Contents

About

Webpage: https://jatan.space/seven-uni-verses-poetry/

First published: September 17, 2025

Seven uni-verses is a pamphlet of poems dedicated to humanity's exploration of the universe. There's nothing quite as bold and beautiful as committing to venturing the brutal colossal desolation that is space. Every (civil) space launch carries not just hardware but hope. The act of exploring the void makes humans special.

As someone who has dedicated his work life to space, I've written these verses over the years to attempt and capture the sheer intensity of emotions and intellectual ambition the cosmos and its exploration evokes. While my poems are intended to be read by everyone, many lines allude to technical concepts for those in the know to savor. A few key references as well as backstories are mentioned in the endnotes.

Accessibility

Open: The Ebook supports multiple accessibility needs, including resizable text, image descriptions, font options in Epub, and multiple devices. There are also diverse formats. Moreover, the book is being offered free of DRM restrictions so you can download it from my website, and consume and archive it in your preferred way. These terms do not support or encourage piracy. Also see copyleft note below.

Ebook first: Reading this poetry pamphlet's Epub or PDF file using a digital device will provide you with an enriched experience since the embedded links are clickable to feed your curiosity and enable discovery. If you're reading this pamphlet physically, or hearing the audiobook, check the Ebook or supplemental PDF later on from the official webpage for your web-clicking convenience.

An ode to our Moon

A blaze aloft at night
sent a glimmer of hope
flying past the desolation

It ignites around Moonshine,
so we can all dazzle
at the suspended blue marble

It twinkles again across the void
for a blistering comeback,
and a tactful splash

Let's keep the path glowing
for these engines of progress,
so we can ferociously return

To our cosmic companion,
like never before.

See poem notes[1]

Our Moon as imaged by the Galileo spacecraft flying past it on December 7, 1992.

Image: NASA

[1] The success of NASA's Artemis I Moon mission, and the amazing views of our Moon from its Orion spacecraft, inspired me to write this poem.

Triple sunset

Here lies the bathing light of the red dragon,
deepening horizons on a world so foreign

Yet much like a haven that is our Earth,
there could be water on its surface unhurt

Could there be life too on this land of the triple-star,
would they also figure out who they are?

Would they comprehend the distant binary-star show?
that they are the suns of the one they know

Oh what a view it would be,
for life there to see

But if on that world
there isn't any,
let it be the carved destiny of humanity.

See poem notes[2]

This artist's impression shows a near-sunset seen from the super-Earth Gliese 667 Cc. The brightest star in the sky is the red dwarf Gliese 667 C, which is part of a triple star system. Image: ESO / L. Calçada

[2] This is a poetic follow-up to my article 'How Isaac Asimov used science fiction to point out our biases'. I've retrospectively discovered that the poem also relates to the vivid science fiction story of The Three Body Problem by Cixin Liu.

Does life really have a purpose?

Space is vast, near-infinite and empty,
but only so much of it can we see

Stuck in a direction of time are we,
and yet we claim how we came to be

Welcome to space-time's infinite array,
where everything lies farther and farther away

Magnificent galaxies may be big and bright,
but their separation speaks stronger than their light

Even the stars are not as close as it seems,
mere little dots that hold distant dreams

Yet even those dots can be the most violent of all,
massive supernovae and gamma ray bursts leading their fall

This is a Universe where the stars are born to die,
some form black holes and to space-time they can lie

Even the smaller stars are hostile in time,
as are their planets that were once benign

Space is cold, and time unforgiving,
space is harsh, and with time it defies living

What is then the purpose of life?
Or are we just a roll of a dice?

Life is purposeless and meaningless,
for every sentient species is ultimately alone
in the vast space-time emptiness.

See poem notes[3]

Image: NASA

[3] That last bit about the lack of time for two species to communicate is a reference to the Fermi Paradox.

Space dreams

a. Our galaxy awaits

The first view of our galaxy awaits,
the lights of billions of suns

Yet each star a destination of its own,
out of reach for millennia unknown

You see, us a species still in cradle Earth,
our ability to spread life still a dearth

Await the Moon, the asteroids, Titan, and Mars,
at all of their dawn but a gaze at the stars

Though without the will and wit to pull it off,
an interplanetary dream by itself is not enough

Need an eye for the details,
a rigor to pick up leftover trails

An incessant readiness for discourse and critique,
and the patience to inspire and teach

All of this is what you possess,
with a forgiving nature, no less

Every such Sol can we not iterate,
and set ablaze life to proliferate

Need but a gravity assist to set things straight,

beyond which the first view of our galaxy awaits.

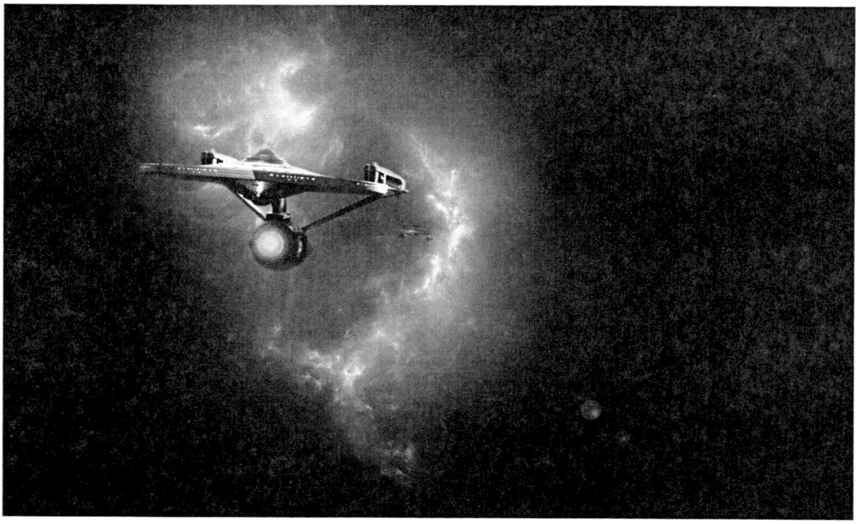

The Mutara Nebula and a Starship. Image: 1darthvader

b. Dream, we must

Dream, we must!
Or risk our species blown to dust

For a future that extends beyond the sky,
the time to act is nigh

An orchestrated descent to the Moon,
and an iterative rendezvous with an asteroid

Carry on with your dream,
and get past the crater's rim

For you have not just the innate curiosity,
but also the warmth of empathy

Persistently crack the seven minutes of terror,
and then be the Solar System torch bearer

A whirl around Jupiter,
and a landing on Europa

A dive through the rings of Saturn,
and a glide above the seas of Titan

The first orbit around mysterious Uranus,
and a swift passage through Triton's geysers

With perseverance and might,

reign in the peaks of eternal light.[4]

This 'family portrait' shows a composite of images of Jupiter and its four largest moons: Io, Europa, Ganymede and Callisto. Europa is about the same size as our Moon whereas Ganymede is bigger than planet Mercury. Image: ESA

[4] "Peaks of eternal light" is a reference to thin sections of near-permanently sunlit areas on the Moons poles due to favorable geometry between the elevated terrain and the near-horizon Sun.

> My first job involved working with some remarkably passionate and like-minded people. I particularly enjoyed spending time with two friends for whom I wrote these respective poems.

VI

Space just desolate...
and yet humans launch hope
to explore some more

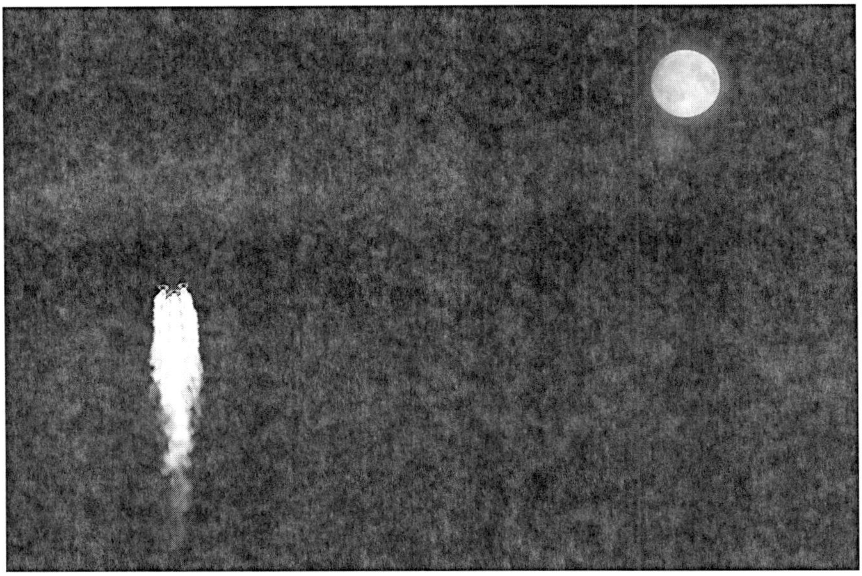

Image: Xinhua

VII

On our Moon

from where the Sun never shines,[5]

a new era will dawn.

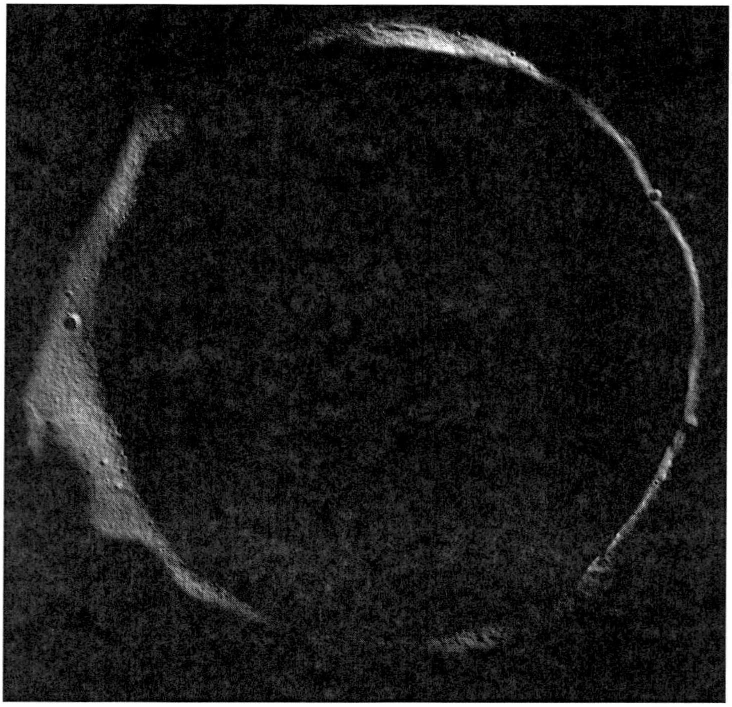

The rim of the 10-kilometer-wide Erlanger crater on the Moon's north pole. The crater floor is in permanent darkness. Image: NASA / GSFC / ASU / LRO

[5] From "where the sun never shines" is a reference to permanently shadowed regions on our Moon's poles which were discovered to host water ice deposits. These could be crucial for sustained exploration of our Moon as well as the Solar System.

About the Author

Jatan Mehta is a globally published space writer, journalist, and invited speaker. He writes Moon Monday, the world's only blog & newsletter dedicated to the exploration of our Moon by countries worldwide. Jatan loves poetry, and has an innate desire to merge it with his first love—space. His space blog and more about his work can be found at '**https://jatan.space**'.

To follow Jatan's articles and future books, you can subscribe for free at 'https://jatan.space/subscribe'.

Support open access

A personal note by Jatan

To support global open access, and in the same vein as my blog, I'm making this book's Ebook and PDF available for free on my website. The book is also listed on multiple online platforms worldwide for $0 wherever allowed. For print versions where the distribution costs cannot be $0, and for platforms like Amazon which don't allow a $0 listing, I'm providing the book at minimum viable prices which cover printing & binding costs, distribution charges, various platform fees, their royalty cuts, and myriad currency conversions. This effort is over and above catering to accessibility needs as well as releasing the core text of my work under a freedom-supporting license as described in the 'Accessibility' section.

Future books I publish will also follow the same philosophy wherever possible :). If you find value in my open access approach and my globally read community resources, kindly directly support independent writing & journalism as a reader: '**https://jatan.space/support**'.

Share your thoughts about the book by blogging about it or leaving a review.

What does space evoke in you?

Write some words, maybe a haiku, or draw. This space is all yours.

9 789334 432558

Printed at Repro India Ltd.